MARK 12, 29-31

29 "The most important commandment, "answered JESUS, " is this: 'Hear, O Israel, the Lord our GOD, The Lord is one. 30 Love the Lord your GOD with all your heart and with all your soul and with all your strength.' 31 The second is this: 'Love your neighbor as yourself.' There is no commandment greater than these."

This book belongs to:

———————————— ● ————————————

The Adventures of Mr. Wilson

A Children's book Series
Series 2

By Dennis and Dolores Horine
Illustrated by Gwendolyne (Wendy) Dean

My humans, I will tell you about them in a while. They sit in this chair with some kind of light. They move the light across the floor and watch Lucky Day chase it, laughing for hours on end. She never catches it. They should call her LOCO DAY!

She is sooooooo odd!
I would never chase that, boring! But I bet I could catch it, Hmmmmmmmmmmm.

Then there is Loco, I mean Lucky Day's Mom, Maggie Mae.

After watching her for a while I can see why Lucky Day is the way she is.

Oh my bananas!

GOOD GRIEF! It is a wonder they have anything left to sit on. Or more important, for me to claw.

Maggie Mae's sister is named BC. BC, now what do you think that stands for? Times up, Black Cat. How original.

Let me show you what she does best.

Now let me talk about the old man cat, Treecat. Yes, that is his name. Turns out he was actually born in a tree. He is very old and moves slow unless it is time to eat. Then he is always the first to the food dish, GOOD GRIEF!

Treecat loves to tell stories.

One story he loves to share is when a large family of raccoons invaded his home. He tells of how he single pawedly chased them out of the house.

Ricky Raccoon says, "hey buddy you ok? Catch your breath then let's do it again! That was fun!"

Mr Wilson says," yea, just taking a break. I like you guys, you are ok. Yea, that was fun."

Well, that did not go as I expected. Must be the Himalayan cat in me..........

Then there are my two humans I let live here. I guess I can call them Mom and Dad.

OH BOY!! First of all Mom.

She sits in this chair for hours with this wheel and spins fur. Who's fur? I do not want to know. When i am sitting next to her I have to watch that she does not spin my fur.

Then there is the Dad.
Dad says, "such a cute widdle kitty. Does the cute widdle kitty want his tummy wubbed?"

Mr. Wilson says," no, the cute widdle kit..... wait a minute, GOOD GRIEF! OK, just scratch my head."

Well, you can see what I have inherited. So much for my nice peaceful life. I know they are not perfect and at times annoying but having a family sure beats being alone. Besides who was going to feed me? I have to admit one thing for sure, ...
....

I LOVE MY FAMILY!

Treecat Publishing LLC
www.treecatpublishing.com

The Adventures of Mr. Wilson

Text Copyright 2020 Dennis and Dolores Horine
Illustration Copyright 2020 Gwendolyne (Wendy) Dean

All rights reserved

No parts of this publication may be reproduced, stored in a retrieval system, or transmitted in any form or by any means, electronic, mechanical, photocopying, recording, or otherwise, without the prior written permission of the copyright owner.

This book is sold subject to the condition that it shall not, by way of trade or otherwise, be lent, resold, hired out, or otherwise circulated without the publisher's prior consent in any form of binding or cover other than that in which it is published and without a similar condition including this condition being imposed on the subsequent purchaser. Under no circumstances may any part of this book be photocopied for resale.

www.ingramcontent.com/pod-product-compliance
Lightning Source LLC
Chambersburg PA
CBHW041157290426
44108CB00003B/96